Yike Song, Gabe Mugroofz's Family Photo Gallery

Yike Song, Gabe Mugroofz's Family Photo Gallery

K. D. Hurley

Forward: Trevor Grayson Clark

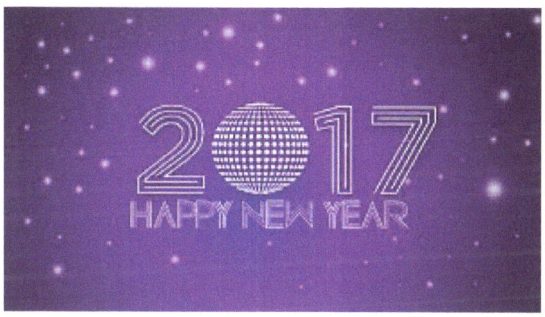

Bay West Hillford & Sherman Smith Books

Victor Page and Mary Trump at Cambridge Version

Dallas. Pichar. Shijiazhuang. Burke. Anhui. Shanghai.

Murphy. Thomas, Abbey. Sanya. Collinsville. Wuhu.

Shen Nong Jia. Sashi. Peru. Kyoto, Xiamen. Tianshui

Yichang. Baoji. Wurumuqi. Harbin. Burns Flat. LoWu

Kunming. Wilson. Chongqing. Juneau. Seattle. Morton

Bay West Hillford & Sherman Smith Books
A division of
Cheekawood HenryBarron Books 2017

Published simultaneously in Italy
Printed in the United States of America

Yike Song, Gabe Mugroofz's Family Photo Gallery

Brief Snapshots on Close Relatives To Sam and Lilyn
/ K. D. Hurley

ISBN-13 978 1542313063
ISBN-10 1542313066
1. Title
2. StevesonRuehan1213.SWCHJ47L84   1997

Bay West Hillford & Sherman Smith Books
A division of First
Cheekawood HenryBarron Books
4830 Wilson Street
New York, NY 10046

14 13 06 22 11 22 08 13   2016 1968 1946 1993 1809 5 4 3 2 1 0

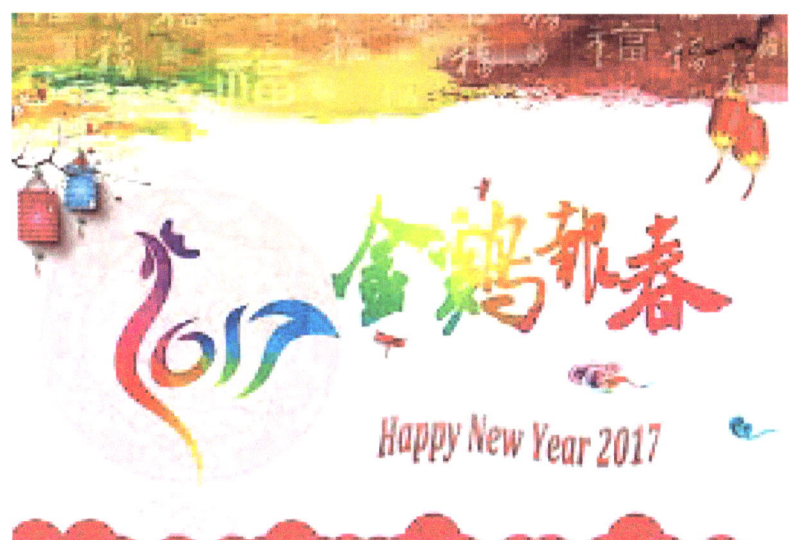

2017 is the year of Rooster, Cock, Hen, or Chick, according to Chinese Luna Calendar, We call male chick "Ji"

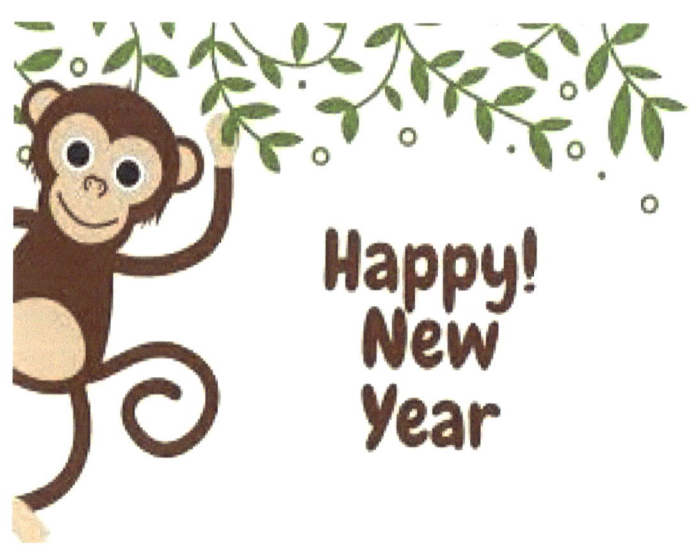

Happy!
New
Year

2016 is the year of Monkey, or
"Shen Hou"
Samrufz Hillford was born August 13, 2016,
To Chris Fine and Amelia Wilson,
Lilyn Cheekawood was born November 22,
2016
To Thomas Woolworth and Abbey Wood
Both babies speak perfect English within
A few days, they are happy gifts from
Silicon Valley

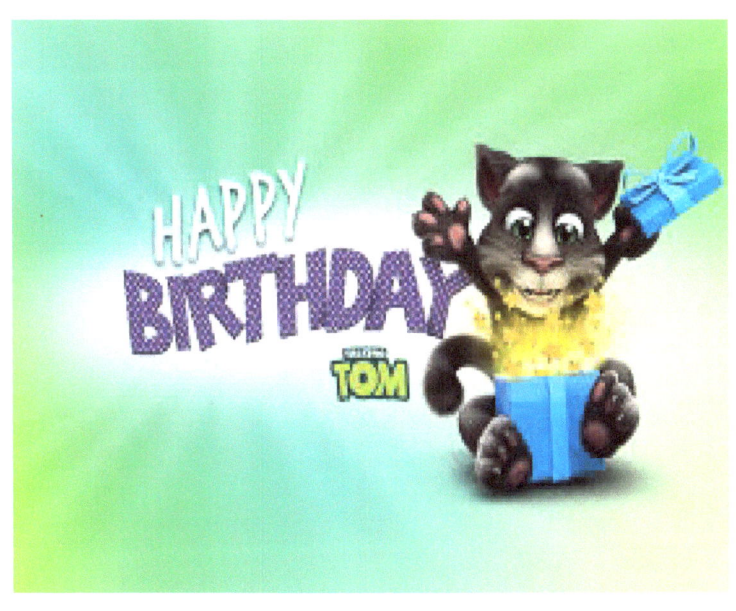

Amy Storm Cats love to say
Happy Birthday to Tom,
Who was born on Christmas Day,
1997, Austin, Texas

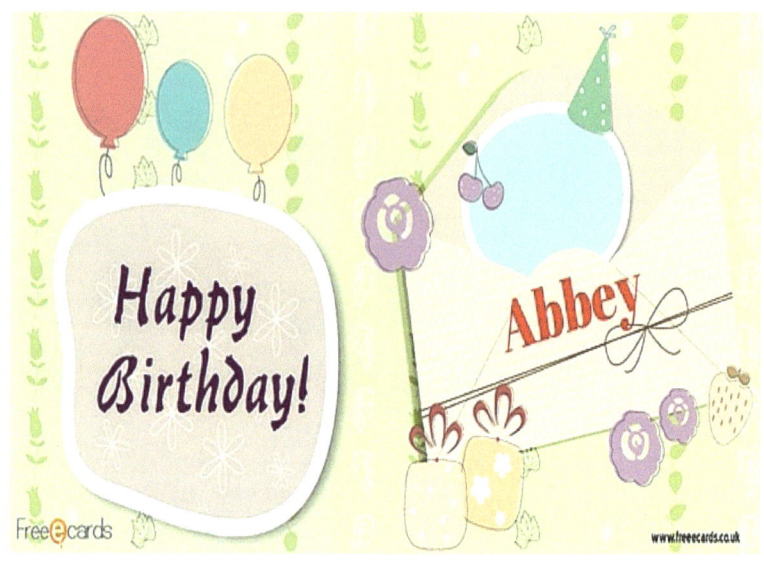

Lilyn's Mom Abbey loves her birthday card,
She is a fabulous woman who carries
Outstanding beauty, patience, and courage,
Thanks to Abbey's sisters Ari Wood, Jemma
Wood, Oliver Wood, and brothers Lucas Wood,
Nathan Wood, and grandparents, Steve Wood,
Patti Johnson from Iowa

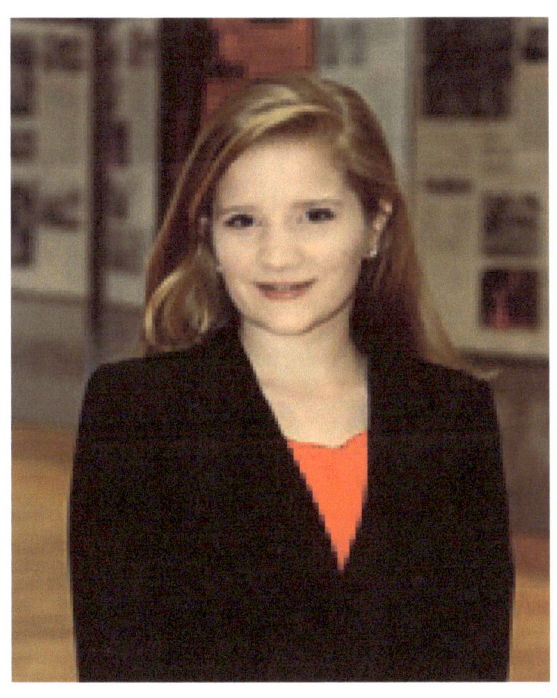

Wed, March 27, 2013 - Congratulations to Amelia Wilson, who has recently been named 2013 Outstanding Senior. Amelia will obtain a double major in Mechanical and Aerospace Engineering. She is a proud mother To Yike Song, Yidi Shui, Yiqiang Wei, Or to Henryetta Wu according to San Francisco, Samrufz Hillford, Emily Hillford, Roxanne Burherns, She makes Stephan Wilson and Kathleen Wilson proud

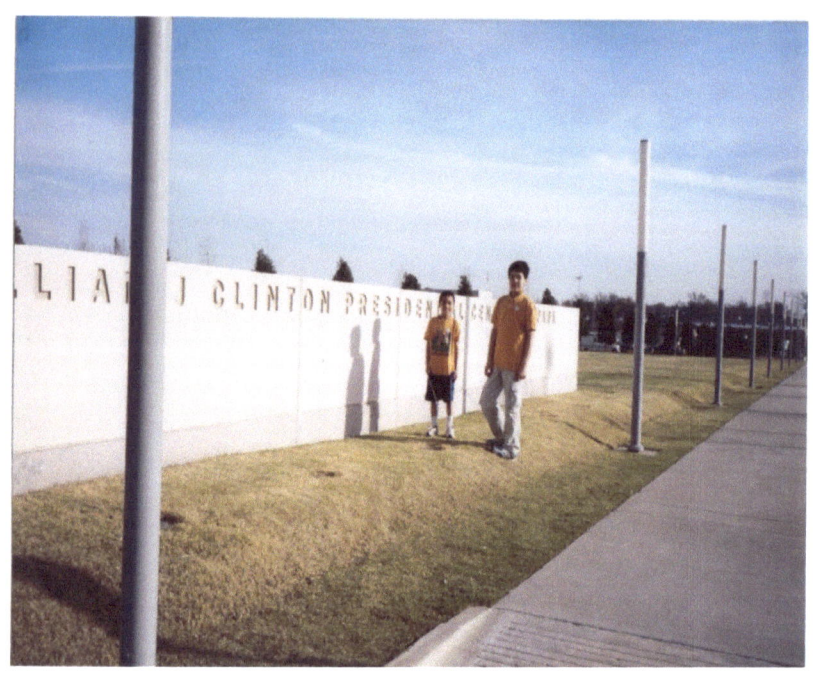

Tom Lee Wu, Sheng Wu, standing near
Bill William Clinton
Presidential Library, Little Rock, Arkansas

Tom, University of Tulsa Freshman, 2016-2010
Sheng, Google softwear engineer, 2014-present

Both love computer science, and enjoy
mountain hiking, and they are adopted by
Facebook, Pixco, Motorola, Microsoft, Yahoo,
Cisco, Google, and Ford Motor

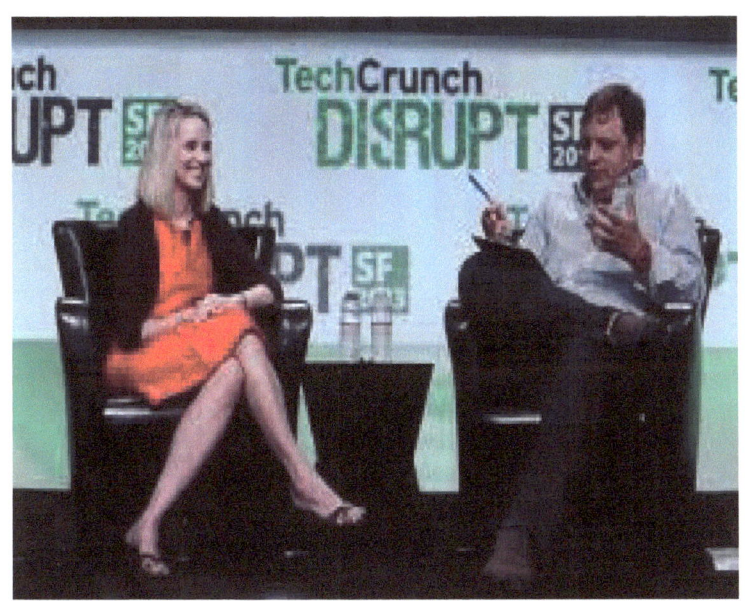

Marissa Mayer and Michael Arrington,
They are hot Ceos from San Jose High Tech
Firm

They do have support to Amelia Wilson,
Sophia Rosenberg, Alex Page, Alison Wu,
Benji Wojin, Elena Murphy, Abbey Wood,
Chris Fine, Thomas Woolworth, and Fei Yang

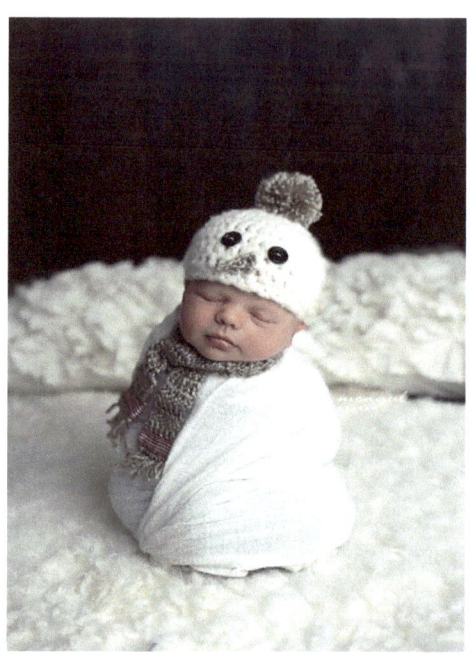

Lilyn Cheekawood, she is precious Both in sixth sense decision making, and in thought provoking speeches, she loves wild wheat field, And enjoys learning from peers,

Lilyn Cheekawood's nick name is Gabe Mugroofz

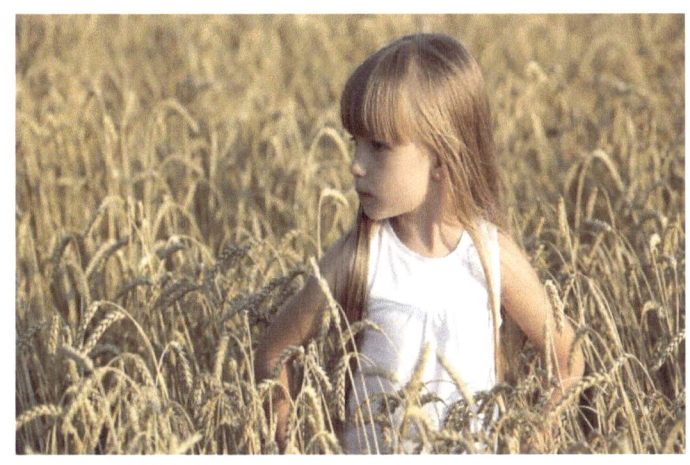

Lilyn Cheekawood, at age three, She makes friends With Aime Wood, Abbey Wood, Tom Lee, Eric Wood, Ji Yan, Shezhi Yan, Olivia Kong, Michelle Overman, Max Barry, Yingfang Yan, Emily Hillford, Arzela Leming.
Emily Krajicek, Gloria Page, Jun Tu, Kathy Campbell, Bing Ma, Leslie Moonrue, Jack Ma, Jay Nixon, Fan Gong, Fan Min, Jing Wu, Ying Liu, She is cousin to Yike Song, Yidi Shui, and Yiqiang Wei, Amy Fowler, Wendy Forest, Matilda Bollag, Max Thelma, Meet Bogue, Marielle Bogue, Aaron Yaris, Sylvan Mayer, Philipine Tucker, Bob Cooper, and Yuewan Peng, Laynie Henry, Anne Raun, Yike Song

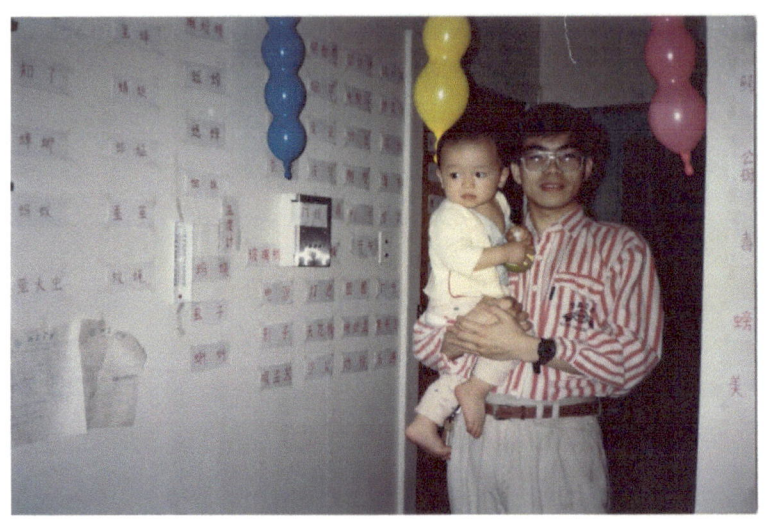

Sheng Wu, Jiahong Wu, on Sheng's
First birthday, May 22, 1994, Chicago, IL

Sheng Wu was born in Beijing Liangxiang
Hospital, pictured above,
Sheng was visiting Dad since December 19,
1993, along with Mother Ji Yan
Ji Yan has a nick name Chinka Whiteson…
Sheng Wu has nick name, Dot, Xiao Bu Dian

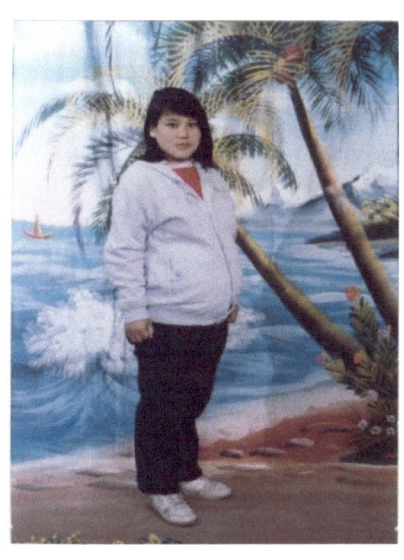

Back in November 25, 1992, when Chinka Whiteson (Ji Yan) Was carrying baby Chris Fine (Sheng Wu), she took a photo, From Grace Brown photo shop, in downtown, Beijing, Muxudi subway stop, near her working Place, which is called Beijing Army and Peace Corp, Reserve INc...she has an undergraduate degree From Beijing Materials Institute, she has friendship With Jun Tu, Xiaodong Xie, Huiju Zhou, Hongjun Han, Hongjian Gao, Lanfeng Yu, Lei Zhang, Qi Wang, Li Cheng, Jian Tan, Donghua Li, Ying Meng, LipingSuo, Jinqiu Tang, Fuchou Fu, Mingfa Wang, Qiuhua Yu, Amelia Wilson, Susan Constantin, Wenhui Wu, Yonghui Dai, Taozhi Zhu, Yu Er Yang, Qun E Yang

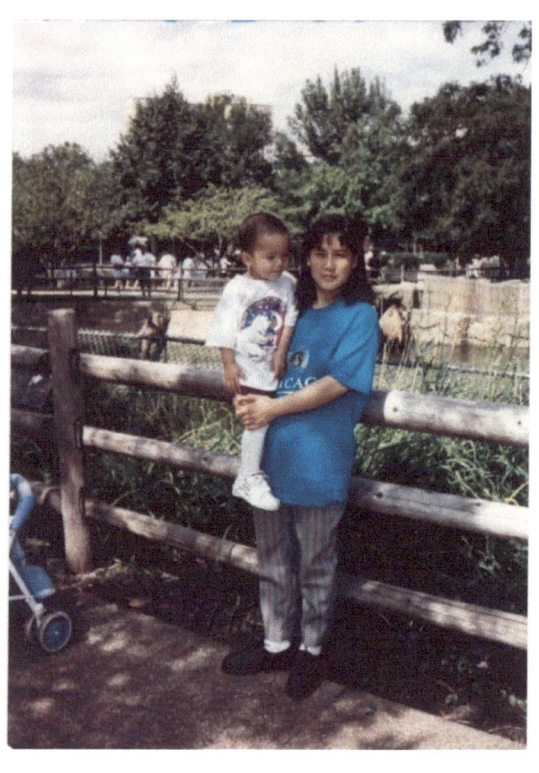

Sheng Wu, Ji Yan, Chicago Lincoln Park Zoo,
may, 1995, They love zoo animals, and
Enjoy fresh air, I bet that Ji Yan
Won't predict that one day, Sheng Wu
Will become Vice President at Youth
and Government via YMCA, Oklahoma,
and actually work for Google, INc.
under Sundai Pichar, and Larry Page
in San Francisco, CA

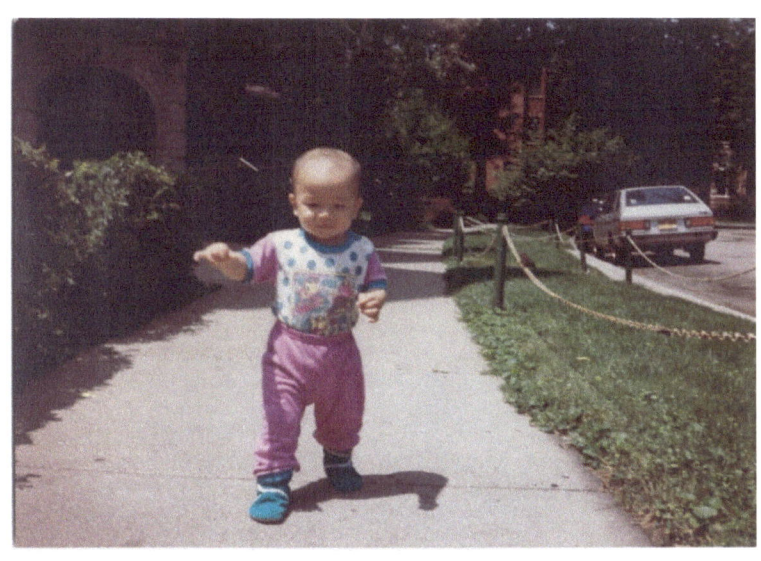

Sheng Wu steps cross Kenwood street,
His first time outdoor, walking by himself,
He truly appear amazing in knowing handwritten
words on Walls made by Jiahong Wu, when asked
which one is Apple, He often points at the right
object, he is famous In Wuhan, Shenyang,
Lanzhou, Changsha, Ningxia, Nanjing, Evanston,
Mountain view, Princeton, and Austin, Sheng Wu
was formally famed by Dequan Feng, and Erin
Zhuo in early childhood Education magazine,
1996, and Sheng learns Chinese, English, Spanish,
and Java very quickly

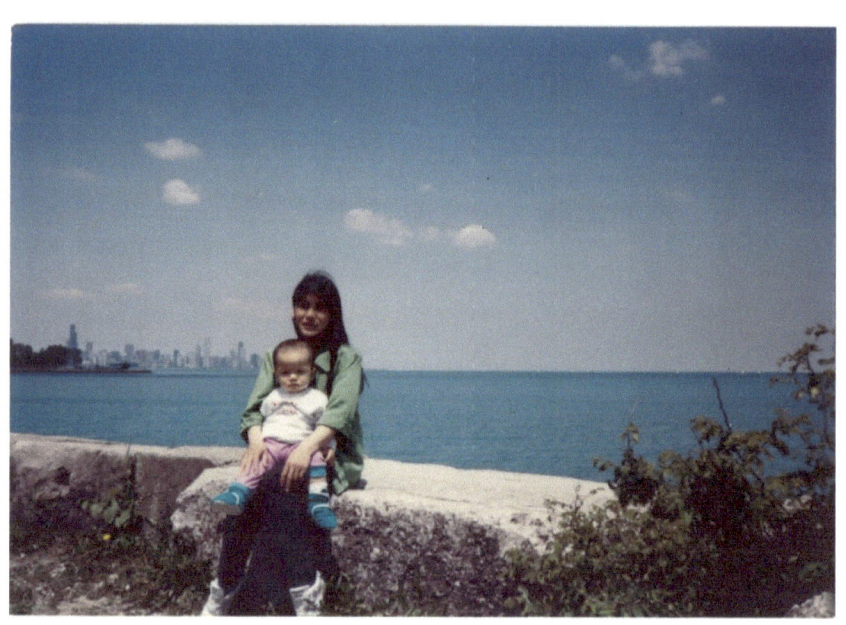

At Lake Michigan Shore, Jiahong Wu
Took a photo of Sheng Wu and Ji Yan,
While swimming in the lake for purpose
Of personal exercise, June, 1995, while
Jiahong Wu works as a P. H. D. candidate
Under Peter Constantin, they have

Zhiwu Lin, Yingjie Liu, Yongming Zhang,
Dehua Wang, Yuhan Zhao, Xiaofeng Zhu,
Li Zhang, Danping Peng, Bing Han, Tao Li,
Tao Zhou, Jiangsheng You, Yan Gao,
Xianghong Gong, Gang Tian, Bing Zhang,
Fanhua Lin, Guiqiang Chen, and Thomas Hou
As math friends

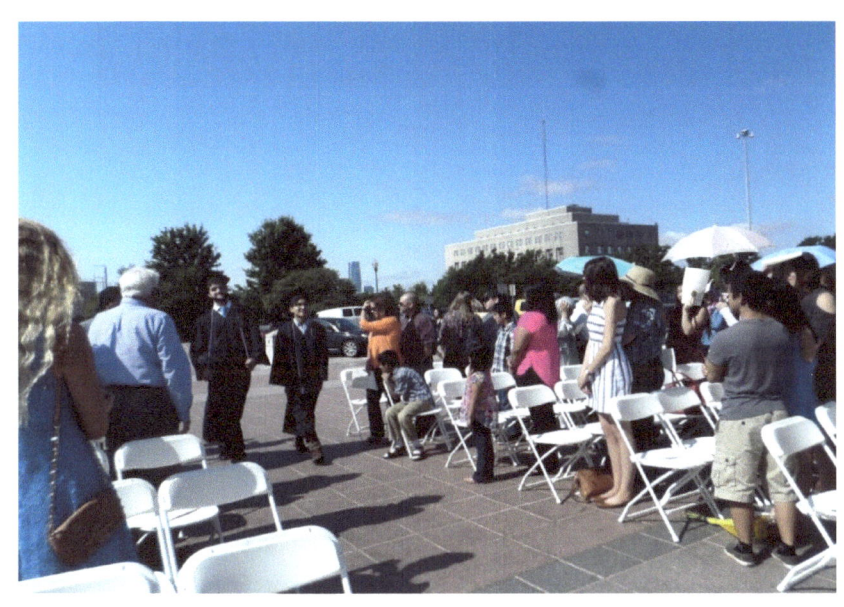

Who walks beside Tom Leigha Wu?
Who is watching June 28, 2016 OSSM
Graduation ceremony?
Where is Chris Shrock?
Where is Jim Hill and Joe Kingery?
Who passes the honor to John Nguyen?
Who steals a look at Abbey Wood?
Who loves her parents as Wavely Wang and
Bing Cheng?

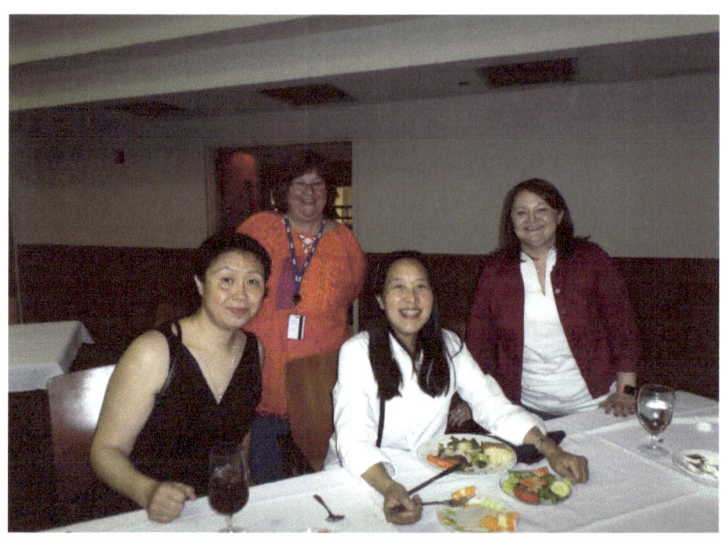

Where is Sue Dick? Where is Mary Fallin?
I spy Rong Yan, Mingrong Rao, Carol Bennett,
And Rebecca Morris, Yet, I wonder who
Is Ruibo Li, and who sets up the tables
With Chuanhui Peng, Daxue Wang, Ji Ma,
Meiling Yang, Jayne Gosney, Hannah
Constantin? Why do Sheng Wu, Amelia Wilson,
Amy Loper, Eric Loper, Tom Sell, Richard Yang,
and Connie Liu care? Why do Chuck Reed,
Angela Zhu, Julia Wright, Asya Peterson, Grace
Lu, Helen Powell, Christina Fallin, and Jessica
Yen mind?

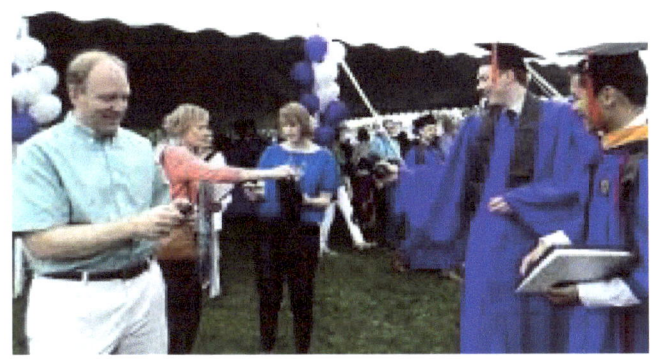

John Lanners, Sally Lanners, and Holly Lanners, They are visiting McCormick school of engineering At Northwestern University graduation party, Students, Brain Lanners, Sheng Wu, Skylar Zhang, Joe Stan, Amanda Huang, Alice Wang, Megan Thielfing, Lee Fan, Pan Yan, Ani Ajit, and Matt Schapiro

Thanks to John Evans, Julio Ottino, Carol Berry, Judith Remington, Mimi Schapiro, Joseph Singer, Rachel Schapiro, Warren Buffett, Kay Baker, Beverly Warren, Natalie Furletts, Bessy Fan, Jiahong Wu, Charles Fan, Ji Yan, Marissa Mayer, Sam Walton, and Pat Quinn

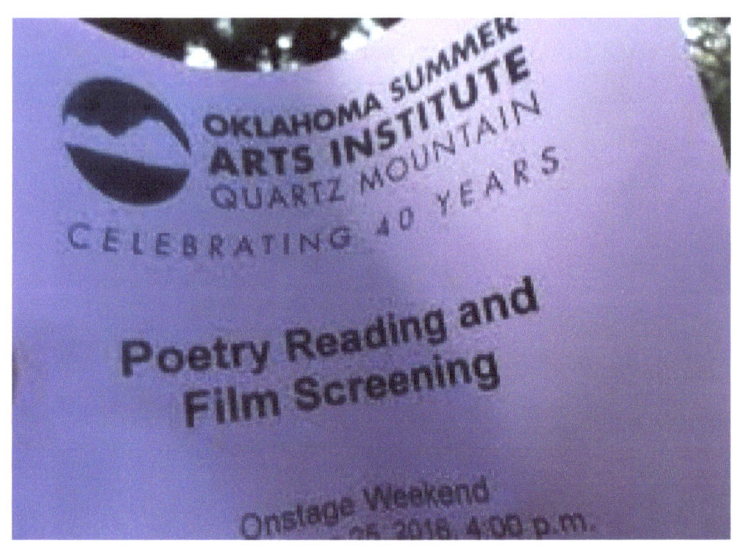

OKLAHOMA SUMMER
ARTS INSTITUTE
QUARTZ MOUNTAIN
CELEBRATING 40 YEARS

Poetry Reading and
Film Screening

Onstage Weekend

Both Sheng Wu and Tom L Wu
Have fun at Oklahoma Summer
Arts Institute, where Julie Cohen,
John Clinton, Jason Grife, Peter Markes,
Ann Peters, Jennifer Hilger, Jennifer Fletcher,
James Lankford, Lee Deney, Cory Williams,
Morgan Henry, Larry Wade, Gayla Foster,
Emily Claude, Laura Deng, Eric Wu, David Lee,
Rebeccak Ellis, Lucy Johnson, Ivan Dai,
Lisa Storm, Amelia Wilson, Justin Wood,
Emily Wang, Grace Lu, Sam Frank all
Enjoy, I bet Abbey Wood has super excitement
When she was chosen to volunteer in June, 2016

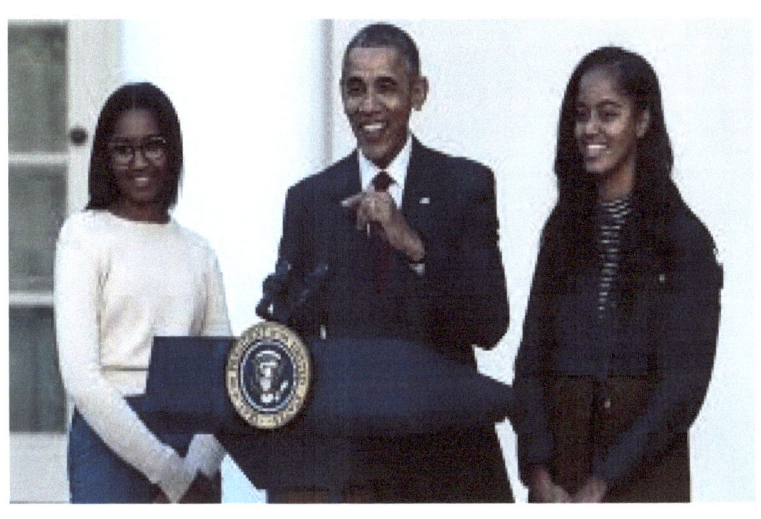

Sam and Lilyn may not know Maya Lin,
Who wins Architecture award on Vietnam
War Memorial design as a college student,
And Who happens to be half Asian, and half
American, but Yike Song and Gabe Mugroofz
must know our president of
2008 to 2016, who is Barack Obama,
He has two daughters,
Sasha (Natasha) Obama (left)
Barack Husine Obama (middle)
Malia (Ann) Obama (right)
Malia Obama is attending Brown University
As freshman, August, 2016

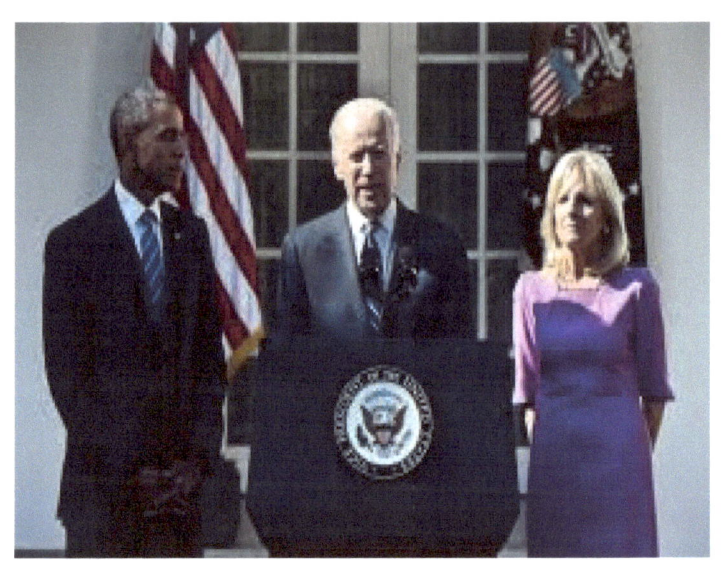

Us vice president is important,
We know from above,

Middle: Joseph Biden (Vice President)
Right: Jill Tracy Biden (Wife to Joe Biden)
Left: Barack Stanley Obama (president)
Unseen: Michelle Robinson Obama (first
lady)

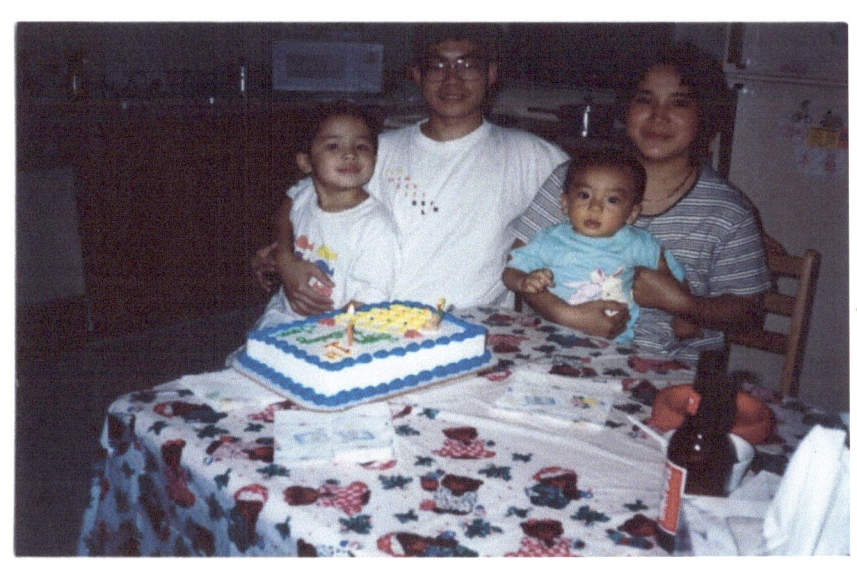

A family of four,
They live in Austin, Texas from 1997 to 2000,
When father/husband Jiahong Wu works as
A mathematician under Jerry Bona, George
Bush,
at University of Texas, mother/wife Ji Yan
works as
Saint James Epochal School Daycare giver
And as Simple Knots INc. bracelet assembler

Left to right
Sheng Wu, Jiahong Wu, Tom L Wu, Ji Yan

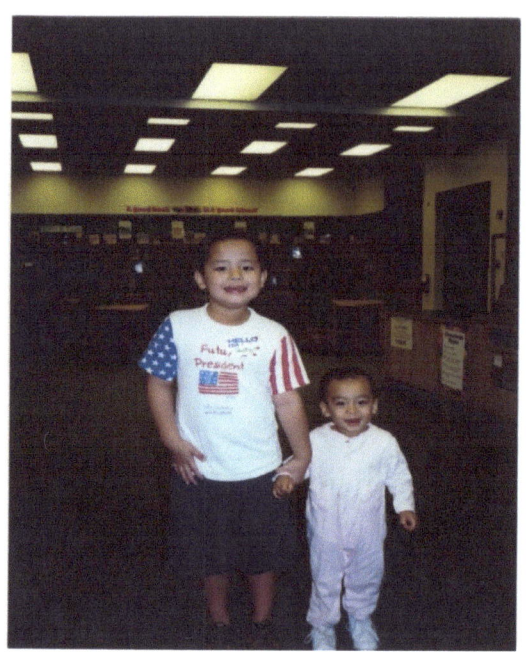

Sheng Wu, Tom L. Wu,
Bryker Woods Elementary School, 1999
Where Sheng Wu, Timothy Lam,
Zhikang Tan, Zachary Lewis Hill,
Amanda Huang, Qinxia Lin, Yali Zhu, and
Ivan Yuan, Richard Chin, Ying Liu enrolled…
Juanming Yuan, Qingbo Huang, Yu Yuan
And Jiahong Wu are friends to Rick Perry,
Hongqiu Cheng, Jun Yan, Siye Wu, Li Yan,
Qun Yan, Feng Suo, and Sijue Wu

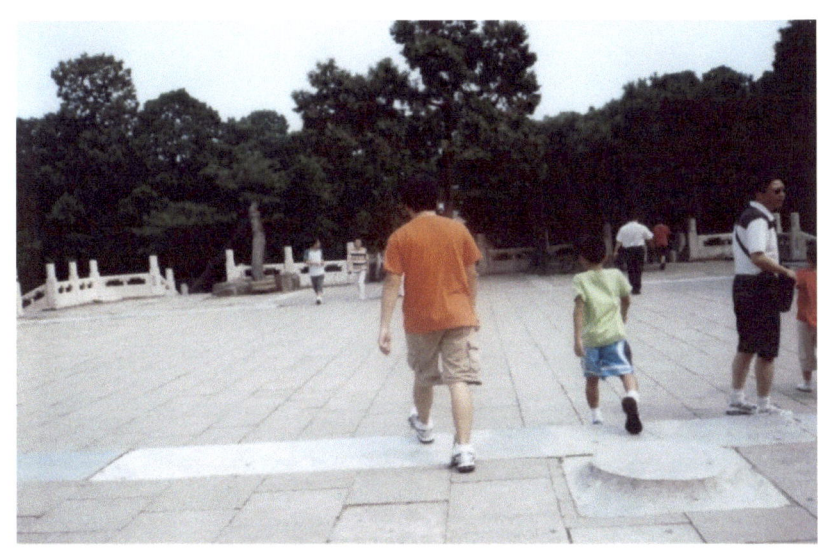

Sheng Wu, and Tom L Wu,

Tiantan Park, Beijing, July, 2007

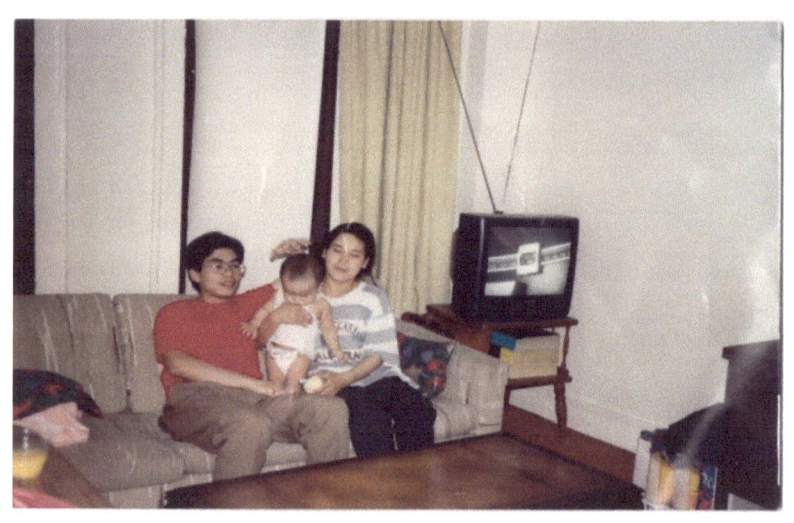

Jiahong Wu, Thomas Wu, and Ji Yan

Jiahong and Ji do welcome their second child to America Thomas was born December 25, 1997, Austin, Texas, Travis county, Women's Heaven hospital, Bee Cave Road, at the time, Sheng Wu Goes to Diving Dolphin Child development center At University of Texas at Austin, until 1998, they love Austin friends such as Hong Jin, Deborah, Theresa Burke, Cathy Lin, Yingcong Tan, Evans Lam, Mariette Coffee, Sofina Yuan, Tiffany Huang, Al Gore

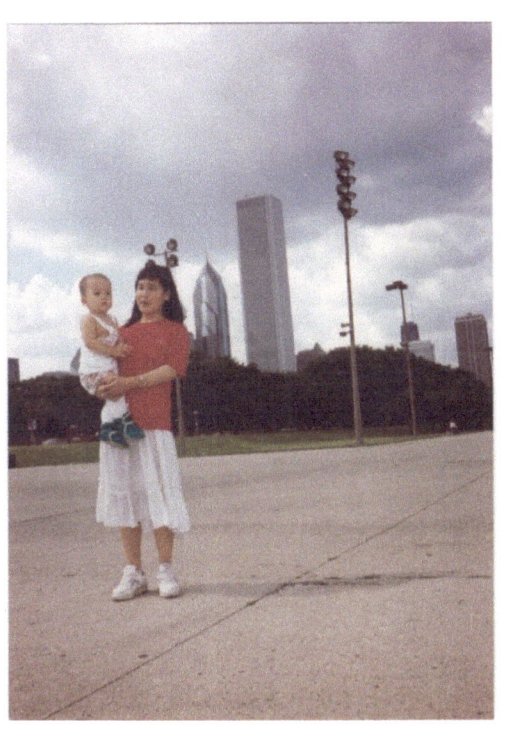

To Samrufz Hillford, this toddler is your
father   Sheng Wu,
When he was small, in Chicago Lake
Michigan shore,
Hyde Park District, and pictured above

Samrufz's Dad Sheng Wu,
Samrufz's Grandmother Ji Yan
Samrufz's grandfather Jiahong Wu

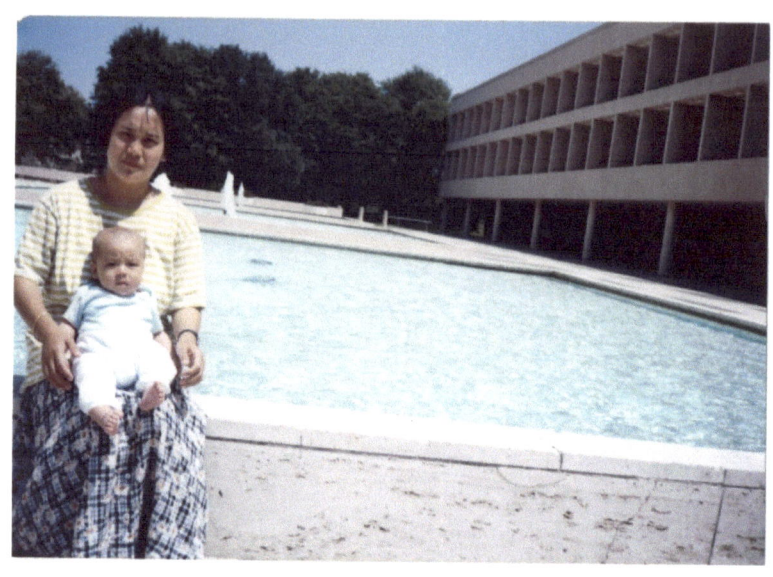

To Lilyn Cheekawood,

The baby is your Dad Tom L. Wu,
picture taken when Tom Was six months old,
at Austin Lyndon Johnson
Presidential museum, Texas, June, 1998

Lilyn's father Tom L. Wu
Lilyn's grandmother Ji Yan
Lilyn's grandfather Jiahong Wu

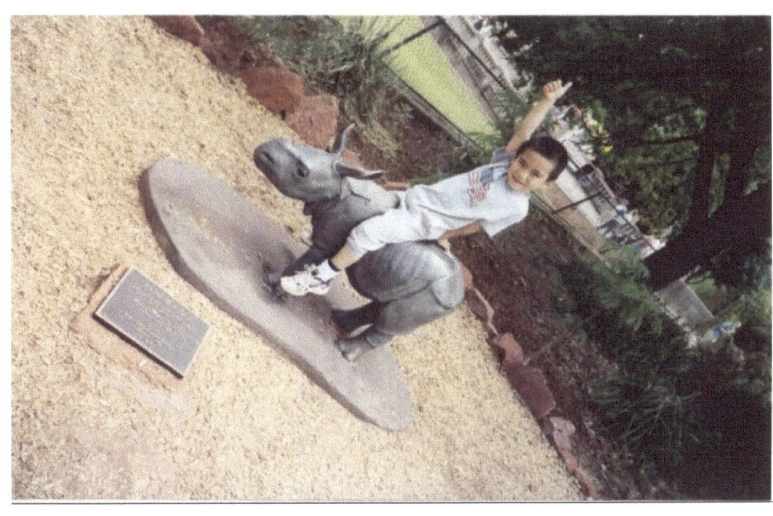

Tom could be cute, cheerful, and relaxing,
When Tom was five, at summer, 2002,

Jiahong Wu and Ji Yan took Sheng and Tom to
Dallas Zoo, where they see lots of wild animals,
They love Elephants, Ostrich, Kangaroo,
Goldfinch bird, Including Leopard, Walrus,
Flamingo, Monkeys,
Hello, Tom?
Abbey and Lilyn wish to have fun at zoo too,
So do Amelia and Samrufz,
Wanna to join them?

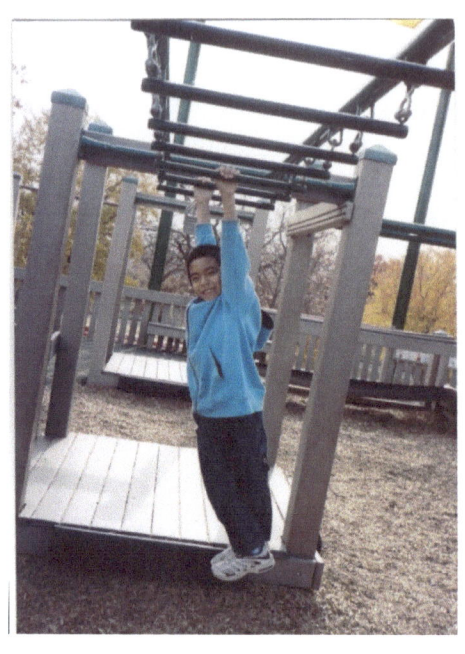

Why does Ji Yan or Aime Wood feel proud of Tom L. Wu? Why does Abbey Wood want to be his girlfriend? Why Gabe Mugroofz or Yidou Juan is curious About Wayne Wood and Michelle Wood, Or about Jiahong Wu and Ji Yan? Nobody knows why, but we do find Tom a Special talent, he swings in Monkey Bar confidently, Believing in himself, embrace Neel Rao, Lucas Wood, Braxton Noble, Albert Cai, Sam Lux, Nick Murphy, Nathan Yu, Mark Gilbert, Benji Wojin, and Chris Raun

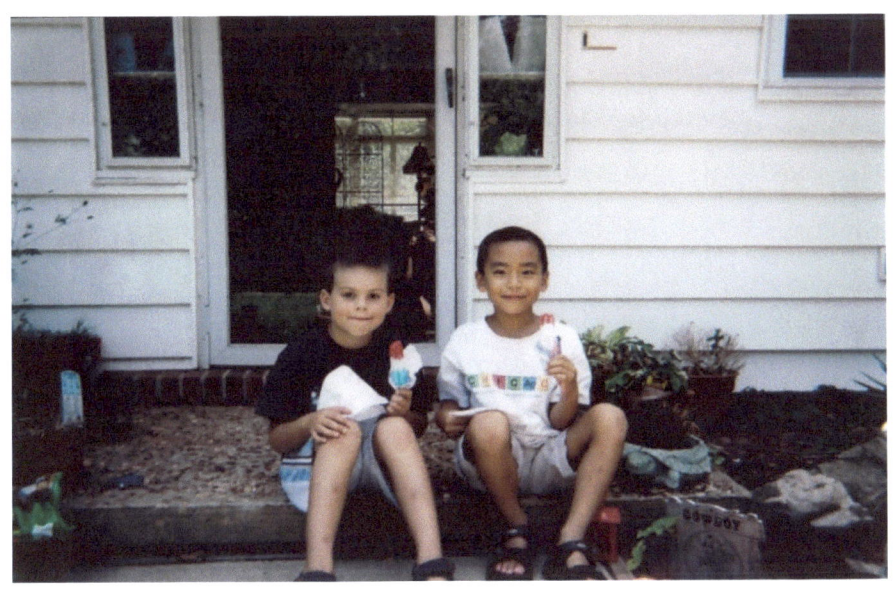

O'Neil Garcia, and Tom Lee Wu,
They are great to each other at
Stillwater Sangre Ridge Elementary School,
When Nicholas Dirks works at
University of Berkeley, San Francisco,
And when Susan Martinez works as
Governor in Santa Fe, New Mexico state,

O'Neil and Tom eating ice pops,
At home of Nancy Garcia, Eric Garcia

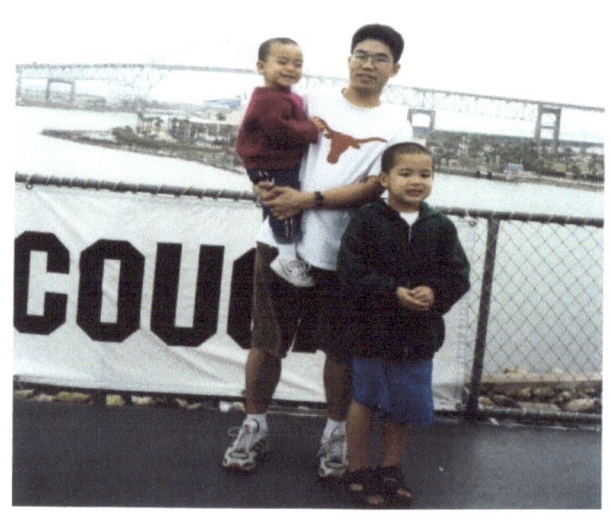

Tom Lee Wu, Justin Wu, and Chris Wu,
Visiting Corp Christi, Texas
Summer, 1999

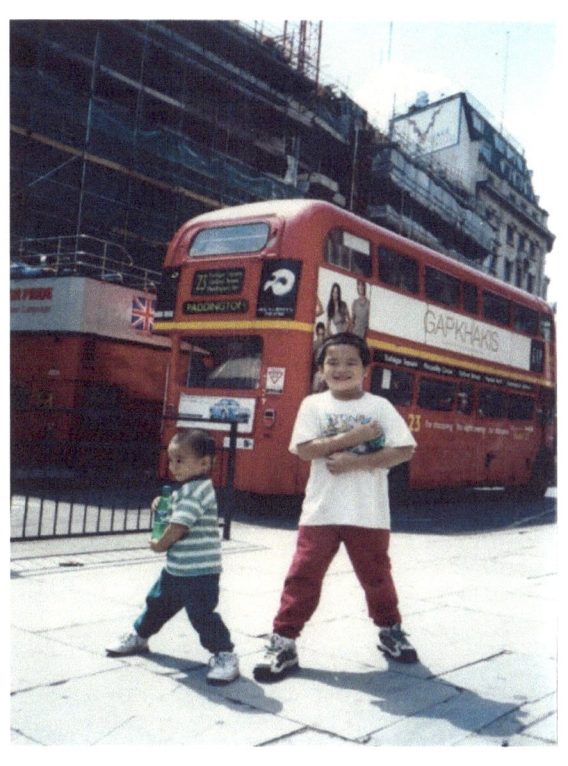

Tom Lee Wu, and Sheng Wu,
London, England, Chinatown area

June, 2000

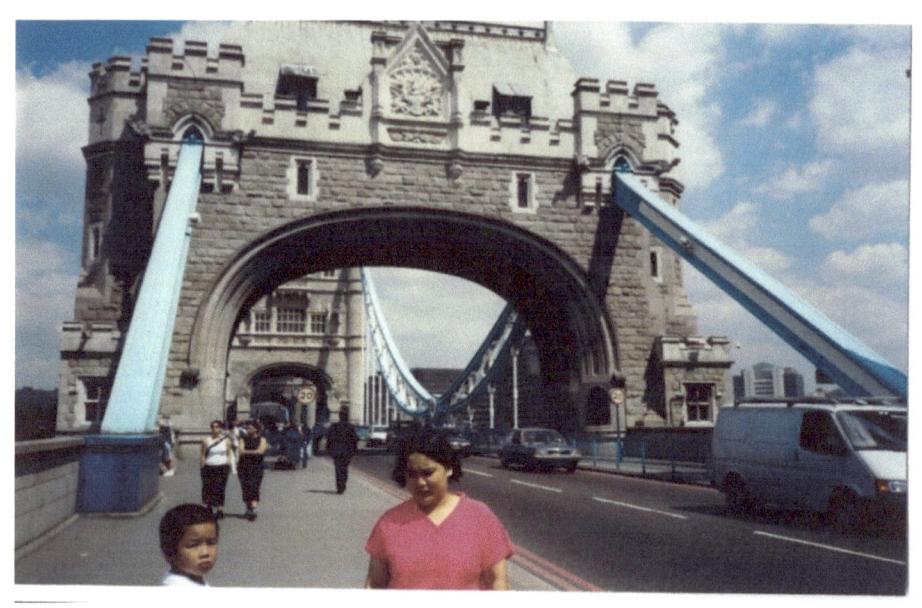

Sheng, Tom, and Ji,
London Tower Bridge, June 2000

They have fun with Elizabeth Queen's garden,
Big Ben, Buckingham Palace,
and British History Museum

Peter Constantin and Jiahong Wu
Were honored to attend International
Math conference, Oxford University

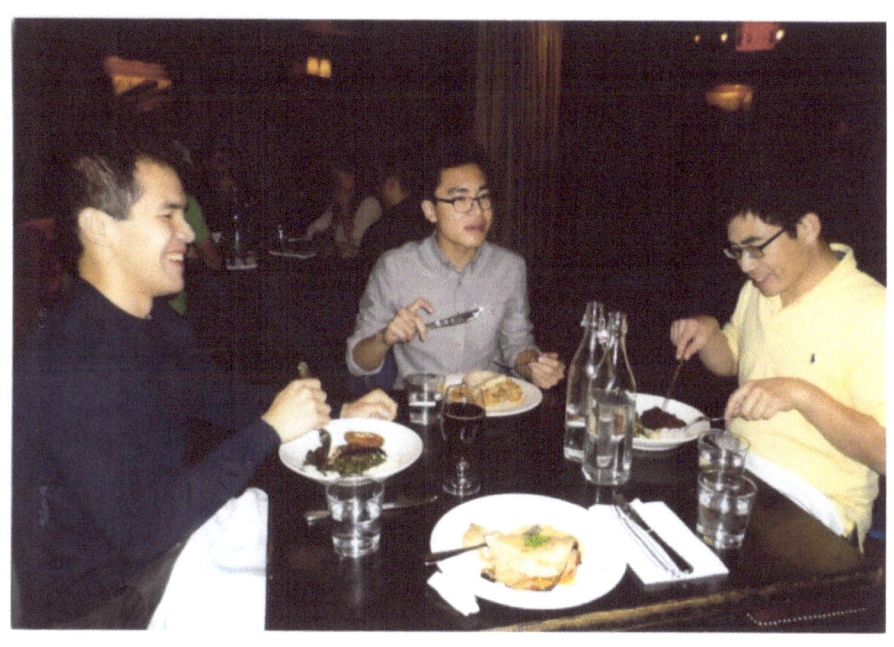

Sheng Wu, Tom Lee Wu, and Jiahong Wu, Ji Yan, Enjoying Thanksgiving Dinner at Russell's House, Boston, MA, 2014

They have done the same dinner as a family of four
at Del More, CA, 2015
Nashville, TN, 2016

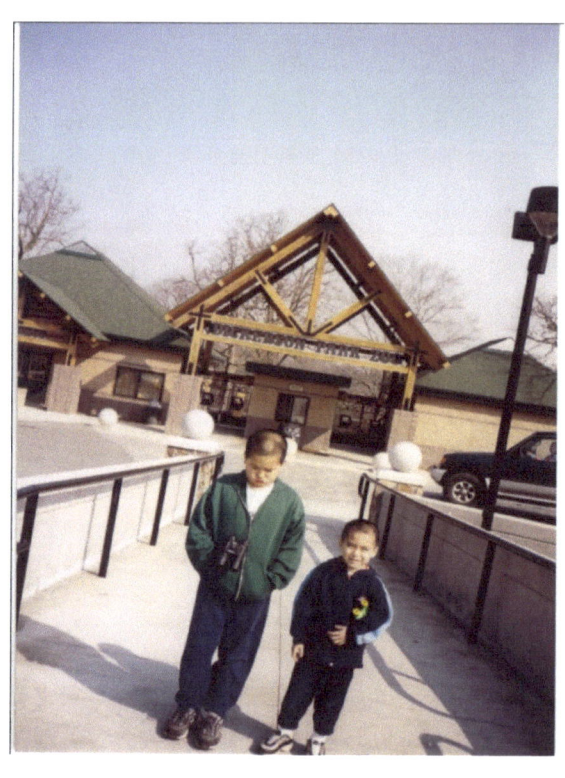

Sheng Wu, Tom Lee Wu,
Brothers with birthdays as 05/22/1993
12/25/1997,

Under parents of Jiahong Wu and Ji Yan
Grandparents of Huiqing Wu, Qiangjiao Kong,
Hounian Peng, Simei Yan, Great grandparents
of Lifu Wu, Zhiyang Zhao, Zhongqiang Peng,
Ju Er Yan, Relatives of Audie Murphy, Jilian
Yaros, Martha Minow

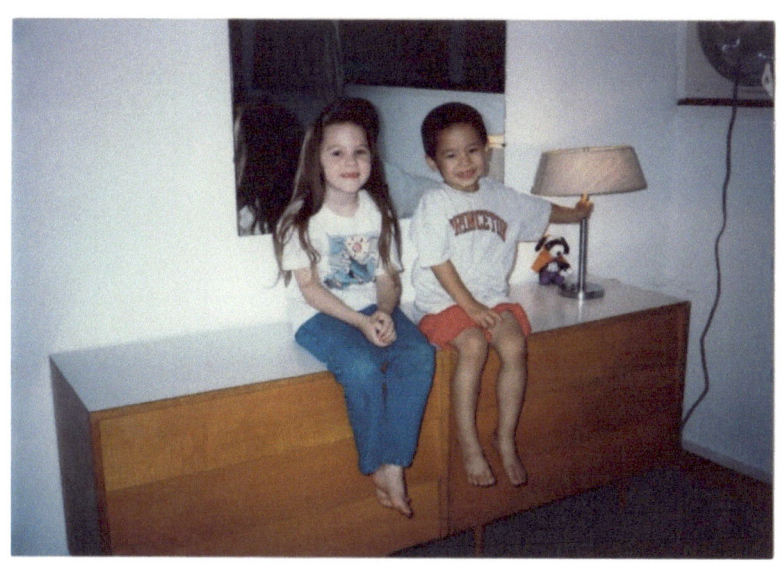

Jodi Jinks (Hui Hui) and Sheng Wu (Dian Dian), Princeton playmates, informal neighbors, between 1996 to 1997, Jiahong Wu has worked at a Fellow at Institute for Advancedstudies, after graduating with a PH D from University of Chicago (1992-1996)

During the period, Ji Yan has been a babysitter To Python Turner, Jack Turner, and Hui Hui, who happen To Have parents as Mark Turner, Megan Turner, Eric Schmidt, and Wendy Schmidt. Sheng Wu, Steve Wood, Grace Lu

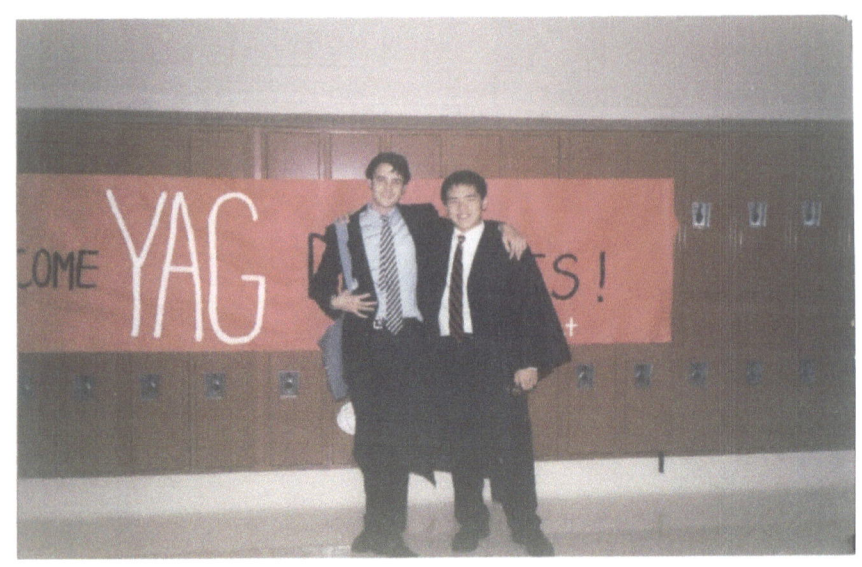

James David Henneberry,
Sheng Wu,
Both member of Youth and Government,
Under Brad Henry, and Todd Lamb
Sheng Wu as a vice President of Judicial ,
Megan Crow, Jim Waldo, Jim Wales, Kim
Henry, Uwe Gordon, John Bartley, Jerry Brown,
Mitt Romney, Edward Lee, Kim Jones,
Stephanie Bice, Stephan Wilson, David Boren,
Barbara Perkins, Zhixiong Fu, Shenghua Peng,
Huijiao Hu,Xin Zhao, Qun Yan, Hong Zhang,
Feng Huang, Mingying He, Jinyuan He, Jiaying
He, Wei Zhao, Zhaoming Peng, Lan Yang

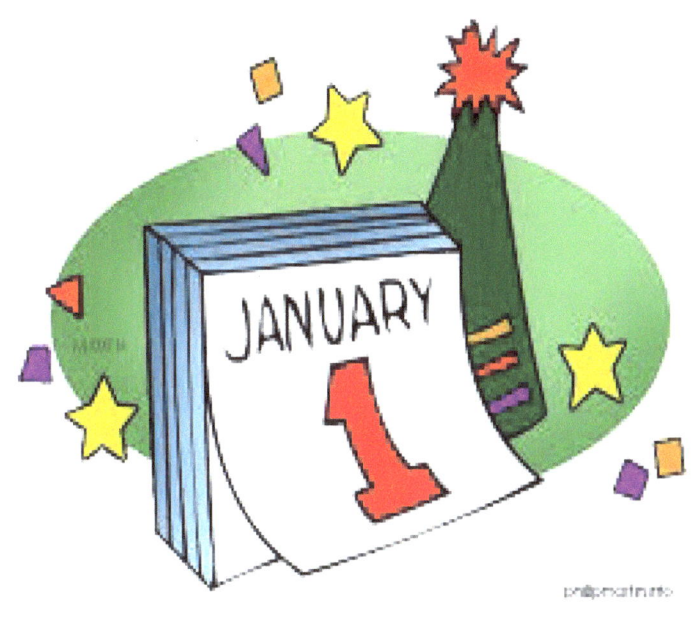

Today is January 1, 2017,
Happy Rooster Year!

Grandfather Jiahong Wu has birthday

01/02/1968, Happy 49th Birthday!

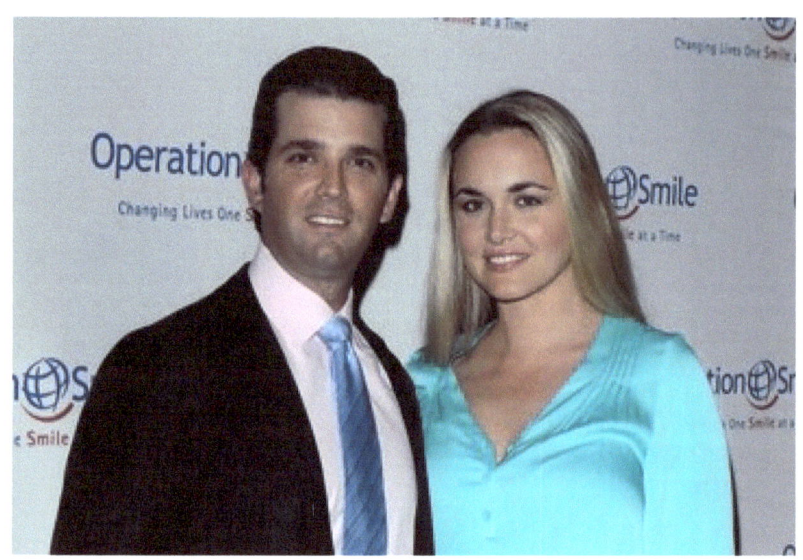
Donald Trump Jr. and Vanessa Haydon

A couple under Donald Trump and Ivana Trump
They are cousins or cousins in law to Jiahong Wu,
Aihong Wu, Ji Yan, Chuanzhen Peng, Yunqing Fan,
Wangying Zhang, Min Wang, Shihe Liu, Bing E Xu,
Lazlo Stein, Rusty Stein, Ann Blair, Megan Barry,
Chelsea Kim, Ray Smith, Michelle Overman,
Jerry Yang, Robin Li, Morton Schapiro, Ai E Wu,
Gerald Clancy, Steadman Upham, Bruce Barry,
Chuanxian Peng, Michael Pence, Karen Batten,

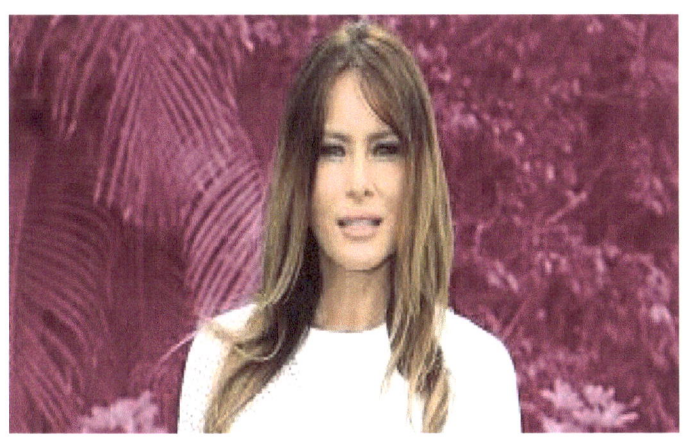

Melenia Knauss Trump, Quinnlan Komng Tuttle
Mother to Barron William Trump
First Lady of President Donald Johnny Trump
She will join the white house
January, 2017

Friends: Paul Ryan, Joseph Shant, Jared Kushner,
Bo Xu, Gangqing Tang, Wenquan Wang, Wuquan
Wang,Shuangquan Wang, Qun Zhi Yang, Qun E Yang,
Jiuzhi Fan, Fengzhi Shuai, Cuizhi Yang, Cai Hong
Yang, Ai Hong Yang, Yao E Shuai, Cai Ping Peng,
And Jialiang Wu, Because Boonie Haydon and
Qiangjiao Kong are sisters

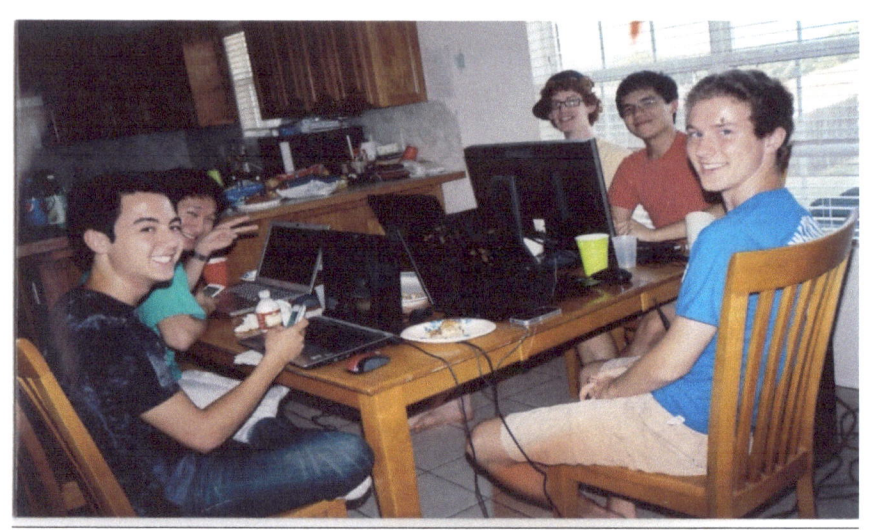

Sheng Wu and Amelia Wilson
Have friends over the house, Los Angeles, CA

They love Samrufz Hillford, Lilyn Cheekawood, Relative to Joy Evelyn Wilson, George Wilson, Matt Wilson,Yuan Kong, Jiezhong Tang, Ken Hansen, Mira Singer, Peng Zuo, Lazlo Stein, Charles Faust, Arzela Leming, Alen Yen,
Abbey Wood, Tom L Wu, Austin Mitchell, Frank Huang,Sifan Zhang, Belinda Mao, Bob Zhang, Benny Wu, Anne Raun, Curt Sharp, Chenxi Wu, Ryan Haas, Qin Yan, Nina Wise, John Wong, Eric Trump, Anne Maples, Barron Trump, Steve Frederick, Tyrek Young, Schapiro Pippen, Phil Jackson, Michael Jordan

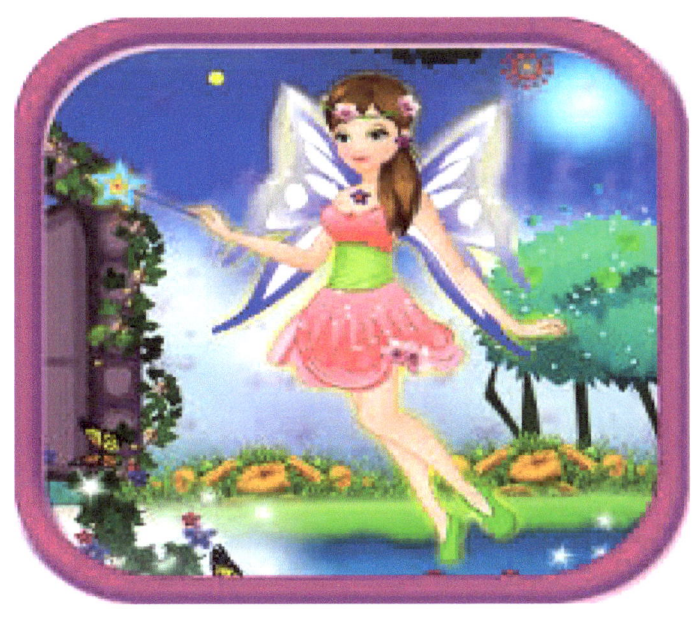

Lilyn Cheekawood is a fairy,
She comes to the world to
Manage her side of Wisdom,
Many thanks to loving parents
Tom L Wu and Abbey Wood
Jennifer Wisdom and Julia Martin forgive you
For being such a strong media!

God bless All
Especially to Jiahong Wu and Ji Yan
Or Mark Wood and Nancy Wood

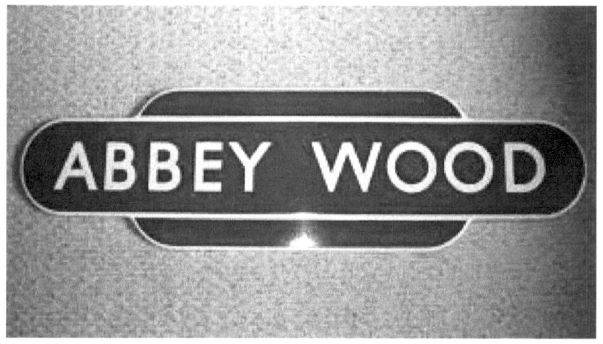

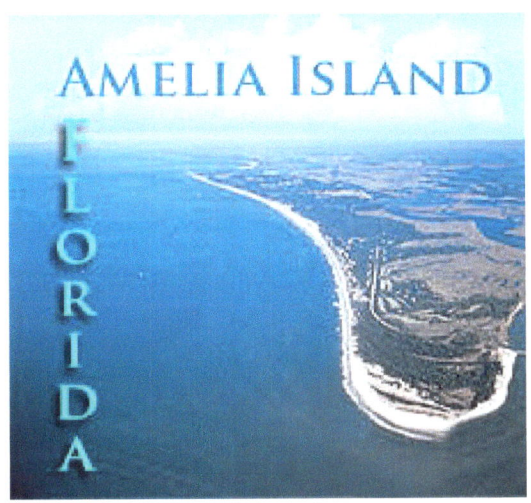